A PALMFUL OF PAIN

A PALMFUL OF PAIN
Nrusingh Tarai

Translation
Dr. Krushna Bal

BLACK EAGLE BOOKS
2021

BLACK EAGLE BOOKS
USA address:
7464 Wisdom Lane
Dublin, OH 43016

India address:
E/312, Trident Galaxy, Kalinga Nagar,
Bhubaneswar-751003, Odisha, India

E-mail: info@blackeaglebooks.org
Website: www.blackeaglebooks.org

First International Edition Published by
BLACK EAGLE BOOKS, 2021

A PALMFUL OF PAIN
Original Odia by **Nrusingh Tarai**
Translated by **Dr. Krushna Bal**

Original Copyright © **Nrusingh Tarai**
Translation copyright © **Krushna Bal**

All rights reserved. No part of this publication may be reproduced, stored in a retrieval system, or transmitted, in any form or by any means, electronic, mechanical, photocopying, recording or otherwise without the prior permission of the publisher.

Cover & Interior Design: Ezy's Publication

ISBN- 978-1-64560-181-4 (Paperback)
Library of Congress Control Number: 2021937175

Printed in United States of America

Dedicate to
LILY

PREFACE

The present scene of the world is a post Armageddon chaos of covid battered mankind where logic moral, philosophical and even political lies scattered in almost all institutions of life. Respect for the Rule of law has been thrown into the cauldron of irrational demands on physical, moral and political territories. In such a scene the poet has two options: rebellion or silence. But a true poet cannot accept the anaesthesia of the heart and sink into a stupor. Nrusingh Tarai being a true poet therefore has opted for protest. But there is no judge at sight. The poet's pen etches out portraits of chaos, moral fall and spiritual hara-kiri. W.B. Yeats' 1916 words prophetically have confronted us with our reality.

The Centre cannot hold
Things fall apart. . . .
The best lack all conviction
And the worst are full of passionate intensity.

The world today has suffered the corona virus, chinese expansionism and recession. As the poet is an Indian he must have seen the irrational protest of motivated groups. The Delhi and Bangalore riots and the thousand attacks on innocence on social media, not to speak of the violation of minor girls. Crime is no more sensational news, betrayal, hypocrisy are our daily bread : In this psychosocial atmosphere a poet frets and fumes in rebellious stance which may appear as mere posturing for in actuality he lives his practised life without a sense of guilt.

Nrusingh has used chaotic imagery, piling image over image to show how decentering and demythologization, dissonance and dissolution have rendered reality unreal :
    Bunch of flesh
    The half blossoming youth
    Is wiped off by the lecherous glance of sinners
Even if you pray with raised arms
Your and our good deeds fail to respond
When would the storm subside ? (The storm)

And
    A bunch of thugs of the fearful dark
    Tear her flesh and entrails. (A poet Asks)

Almost every poem is a protesting cry against the moral fall of man.
Nrusingh Tarai has shown promise in his poems. I hope he develops a vision of man rediscovering the lost values. More care should be lavished on versification for the verse liber is easy to handle but difficult to master.
I wish Tarai all success in life and hope his poems attract the attention of the discerning readers.

Prof. Prafulla Kumar Mohanty
'Chitrakabya'
Sishu Bihar, Bhubaneswar - 24

JOINING THE ISSUE: TRANSLATOR'S RIPOSTE

In the wavering, waning daylight of Dec. & Jan nip, as I sat lunched over my reading desk browsing through Nrusingh's sheaf of poetry I was, to understate, struck by their soreness, clarity & missive. I was even beguiled by their native rhythm, nuances & amplitude & range. There was an empathy for the underdog, the dispossessed & disinherited. There were flashes of recognition that there exists, yet, an overweening sense of beauty & joy that exhilarated me. I tried to convey as much of the original as possible in translation. And all the same, I was confirmed in my suspicion that no translation can be definitive, unilateral, monolithic, unicellular. What I wanted to do was what Tagore had done in rendering his magnum opus into English. The rendered ones are at best a homage to the original. This is what the translator of Neruda averred. When I contemplated over these wide-ranging thematics & poetics Odia language & rhythm & cadence & lilt were in the air. I could imbibe it as I encountered the multilayered connotations. The waves, the blue vacancy, the efflorescence, the rains & the damp created an aggregate dimension. The reading between the lives defined my experiential awareness of the narration, the modulation.

Some of these poems are a little tightly wrought. Some hang about a whit loosely around their staple premises. In a few poems, the seminal theme or metaphor holds the diffusion together while in others the primal intensity dissipates into the elongation of rhythm. In 'Identity' the revelation tokes the poet by surprise. The dips & hollows, the eddies & whirls, the boom & slump gather the whole of life's fabric into unison, he realizes. There is an interface with cussedness, callousness, cruelty & privation. And he is left high & dry finally with an indecorous, ignoble, unheroic identity, joining the bandwagon that munches to the tune of ideological claptrap & shibboleths. This vein of realism would, one is persuaded to believe, make him a cynic, a dyed-in-the-wool pessimist. But in 'An Autobiography' the asserts his modesty with a kind of undiminished non-chalance. The panache carries the poem through to the end and although it has a muted denouement, his hopes & aspirations came through with vividness, even alacrity. The whole sack of realism receives a repeated beating. Thus, his private dreams & public persona get implicated in an internecine rift. The fug-of-war, the tension, the rivalry of impulsions never ceases. There is no consolation in terms of retreating into half-way house. No compromise & no resolution. The barest of insensitive tangibles is what the poet braces for. This vouchsafes for his dogged refusal to kowtow to complacencies & half-truths. And yet in the body of poetry he makes his own statement.

On would wish with the evolution of his passage, he would revert back to a native longing for small happiness & joy. Meanwhile it is an unremitting wrestling. As I did the rendering through, I found myself overwhelmed by their anxiety & felt like echoing a zen koan in the manner of Neruda's translator, Alastair Reid- 'In this net it's not just the strings that count / but also the air that escapes through the meshes'. So be it with this.

BBSR, Sailashree Vihar   **Dr. Krushna Bal**
Feb.15,2021

ACKNOWLEDGMENT

My sincerest thanks to Dr. Krushna Bal for his very adroit and imaginative handling of my poetry while translating them into an alien tongue – in effect it is no more that alien and takes after the original mode and manner.

My heartfelt sence of gratitude goes to Prof. Prafulla Kumar Mohanty for his appreciative introductory note to these poetry. He has brought the very nature of poetry through his footnote.

My thanks also goes to Sj. Duryodhan Parida for taking pens to correct the drafting and see it through the press to the finishing shape.

-Author

A CONFESSIONAL

Sometimes it in a resurrection of light
within life's expansive borders
or love's spread
over the infectious limits of pretensions.

The friends of my life
get soaked in the exuberant waves
that rise sevenfold
among tears & blood
or a life that gets intoxicated
In the blowing of flowers & spring
Light & shadows play hide & seek
Life the sunlight & shade
Covering the consciousness anew.

The words touch me life the
sounds of a conch shell
keep touching every hour of sensibility
I get expanded
And create the words
In a long interregnum.

This proximity to poetry
Becomes my identity.
I have seen it from infancy
Its dream & offered my obeisance.
Its touch & belief have lent me

a new commitment of feeling
new idiom & new habitation

The loving commiseration
& images of many eyes
& many a heart.

Sometimes it becomes a fragrance
or a bewitching belle
or a premise for living
an offering of love.

I go searching for a passage
longing for a fresh down
for the language of man
& joy of liberation
seeking amity & an intimate bosom
The spell of writing overpowers me.

The acme of consciousness
gets illuminated
In the sharp, biting lyrics
And the mirror of senses
turns grey like afternoon
The foot marching forward
In the deep dark of suffering
To write the chronicle of
a thousand agony
to compose hundreds of
powerful poetry
To dislodge the burden of pain
from behind
Poetry blossoms

creating a citadel
of aristocratic words.

I dream of madness
The placid, beauteous surface of earth
And the auspicious hymns of
life's conch shell
Where images collect
dense, precise,
strange aesthetic of
customs and faith
And the galaxy of rainbow tails
usher creation &
its probabilities
The possibilities of dialect
& belief thereof
And the regurgitating sources
of life in words after words.

The sea-green waves, the twittering's
of fowl
The scent of flowers & the depth
of palm groves
The redolent being of spring
The dream drenched nights
The beautiful, enchanting sights
of mustard yellow,
The rivulets, green woods & hillocks
The images of far horizon
Divine minstrelsy overcoming all
Everything belongs to mans earths
& the cadence of my poetry.

Nrusingh Tarai

Epigraph

'In my limbs, life, be fruitful.
Cultivate me with your South.
Sun assist, and sapiet Love
Through my buds and branching move.
Let the words add on my mouth
The inner to the outer whole.
Grant me time, place, peace, affection
To ripen into your perfection'. (Elegy)

-Stephen Spender

CONTENTS

The Storm	19
In captivity	24
Preliminaries	26
Album	28
No Clouds in the sky	30
Duryodhan	32
Flowers of stone	34
An Evening in the city	36
The River mirrors the sky	38
The eyes of Dark	39
Cuttack	41
The Rain storm	43
Jharana Pothala	44
Surrender	48
A poet Asks	50
Redolence	51
Two metaphors of love	52
Night	54
The Goddess	55
Of me	57
The Role	59
The Unknown Man	61
Time for Building	63

Offering	64
Descending unto the Earth	66
No clouds in the sky	68
Passer-by	70
Ascension	72
Poetry : Thou Hast no peers	74
The Sunlight	76
Death	78
Silence	80
Seven Rounds to a Dream	82
Irony	85
Mask	86
Identity	88
Destination	90
Cover	92
The spectacles	94
The face across the windows	96
As I looked back	98
The Afternoon sky	100
Obeisance	102
An Autobiography	104
Debaki	106

The Storm

The thick, layered saffron
In the pitiless afternoon
Wrenching the whole body with exhaustion
The place, declining rays
Create a storm amid the occidental sun.
Scalding the lips of the clouds
with bold stripes
It is moonless dark in the sky
And the parched soil.

Like a long sword the storm rises
Through the passage to the village
and in towns
And the rocky hills and borders of the pathways
The soil on the brim of paddy fields
And at the brick-kiln and
Where the summer corn grows.

Baking the whole body to pieces
Skin & bones
The palmful of blood offers the oblation in the sunbath
The vain nor'wester likens to a jungle python
Clots of blood &

bunch of flesh
The half blossoming youth
Is wiped off by the lecherous glance of some sinners
Even if you pray with raised arms
Your & our god fails to respond
When would the storm subside ?

The panting hard, desperate
like the panting at the end
Panic & endless dread
dark and desolation & shrieks
The circle of typhoon envelopes the whole.

Like a wild undergrowth
Like stray thistles
The wooden wildness
encircle the unkind sky
And the restless, pallid clouds.

The storm rises once again
On the back of the declining sun
Burning the human hearts
Trees & woods, home & hearth
hills & rocks & forests.

The hawks & silver kites
Are flapping their wings in flying
In the plenitude of vacancy
Wiping their fishy beaks
And shaking their moist plummage
Sullen, unsoft body.

And you go questing for away
And I would go pining for freedom
Each of us seeks and seeks quiet
To be spared the queries
Culled from woes & anguish.
And the girl in class eight
becomes the unwed mother
Whose business is it anyway,
And Sukkah Sethi squeezed in the vicious cage of caste
Retreats from the temple, precincts ??

She does not retrieve that evening
Taapoi keeps searching
Lost in storm & rain
In the rain-lashed forest
Deeming it as her sanctuary.

The storm rages in Kandhamala
Nandigram, parliament &
Assembly house
And it also shrieks in famished body
and hungry stomach.

The storm breaks in the respiratory pipes of Singur
The liquer den, black money, chit fund
And on the luscious lips of the blooming virgin
She also moans in Godhra Rly. Stn.
In reprisals, hatred and intolerance.

Tearing apart the eyeball of the sky the rainbow bore
If would gather the earth from below and light from above
And would, as if, the liquid & fatty meat

through its mouth from the mother's breast
In bouts, pouncing & bouncing
And all live ecstasy would die
In a moment.

And so much of lowing would wither away like thunder
from the azure vacancy into the earth
And man's supplications
his tears & blood
The reverse flow of the sea
like blood
So much of grievance
for rice and rice water and spinach
For Karma and Dharma and Liberation

The storm would blow over like its own
And carry along
the pebbles, soil, rocks and sand, blood & flesh & bone
Corpses & coitus
And all live colours of life.

The drains & mud-silted
Like putrid meat illimitable
And stabbing my chest & back with stones
And the storm would pass away
lighting the pyre
of my gathering dreams

Shakuntala & all the faithful women
Would throw away the apparel
draping their body
And would be suffering the pangs of estrangement

Would paint the bodies with insignia of lust
And hunting in troubled waters
for the scales of fish, snails & conch – shells
The wavelets restive.

Who would reckon
In the storm's wake
Who survives & who do not
Who is prostrate on dust
And how much wherewithal & life is lost
The beggars & destitutes
The proletariat would be looking for
the corpses of their oppressor.

The storm would lick away all the raindrops
all the thirst
And wrap off the pristine chastity from the winter's brow
And all the sweat & sun & shadows
from the summer's seas
The flow of life.
The pace would land
So much of pain & agony
In the wings of the storm
And the smouldering ember of resentment
And my pain drenched life.

The storm might uproot the towering stem
The infidelity & blindness
And can wreck the vain self
That has been nurtured long
And all the stubbornness would give way
All the sins, evil, injustice & rocks of sin.

In captivity

The exhausted body
Sweats profusely
Without any let up.
The undone jacket is soaked in smell
And some lingering irritation.

The unendurable heat
beneath the sky's bowel
The sharp twitterings on the rims of the passage.

The sun & the winds wrapping it
are getting sizzled
In sulphurous heat.
The tender foliage carries
the stench of sweat & laceration.
And the sunken blossoms give off
the disinterested passion.

The rains are failing despite its efforts
The thwarted longings
of the floating clouds
fail to melt.
The birds feathers do not find it easy.
And the bride wails
bidding adieu to her parents' house.

There is a tiger sitting on the way
And a Ravana on the throne
The helpless Baula
Turns to a stone
for the upkeep of truth & Dharma
And the lusterless vision of
the captive sky.

Preliminaries

The rain-drenched skies
of seven colours
The leafy soil
And all those remembrances
that have washed leaving footprints on earth
Three quarters ground, and two layers of time
And the floor moist with scarlet blood
that has been shed
The vision of blood streaming everywhere.
The feet & palms are bruised and bleeding
and the bloodied faith
That is the poet's dream.

The pride of acceptance
All those blood and tears
And the assurance of admission
the lust for ache
Sometimes the detachment
of quest casts its spell
In the sacred flame drowned with
Sexual orgy
The enraptured soul
in the intimacy of absorption
To pluck the rains from among the poison
We owe it to the poet.

The agony that rends the eternity & buns it to its marrow
The shriek of a faithful soul & commitment
The droplets of rain
The tiny being & darkness steals in a moment.
That's the illusion of life ......

The intimate sky bows down before illusion
The dead bones quicken into life in soil
And the spring breeze caresses the lifeless bones
Congealing the words.

The poet's vocation
Is questing for a plunge into otherness
and love for the objectivity
The insane looks for the truth that's hidden
for the belief that has vanished
The pining of the river & hillocks
And the idiom of man
in the lips of the flowers
that are a tremble.

Album

All the current, stream and tune & rapture
Are congealed.
Like the quiet cold blue
Drops of blood & tear
Have left a coat, breastful.

Drops of rain dropping on Kakudi creepers
And petals of Jahni flower
Like Monica's yellow, mildewed cheeks
The waves are slumbering
Beneath the long eyelashes of the azure sea.
The mind is a tremble
And fragments of flowing waves are stilled
All on a sudden
One never knows, how
just like that

The sea of tears
And the haphazard, trembling
Unstable footprints
On the banks of the sea
And the innocent, moist Shravan gets imaged in the eyes,
And waits for a day that is yet to come.
Mentally visualizes the form
In the borders of the sari

Or in the veil of the lips
To tie up the being of the lovers.

The dense dark
her love is like the countenance of dark
like the wan moon of the dawn
And yet it comes for a wok
Scything a scar
the refrain of agony.

Be it weal or woe
The feeling loses its way
The faded photograph
Sees its own in the flow of the spring
And pines for intimacy
In the floating clouds
And memory turns to become a painting.

No Clouds in the sky

If you want to see
how the vision within me is imaged
In the erotica of green
or in the arid stretch of sounds.

How do the fronts of the four sides look
the scare on my bow
the grounds beneath my feet
The winkless pair of eyes.

O natives of the cities,
Why has not the lotus of love blossomed here
And the Zephyrus has not stirred
And the green woods are excluded from vision !!

Death beckons me come hither ......
And dreams harken me ....
And life summons me ……..
And pain points its finger ....
The anger of the mid-sky coated in smoke and dust
paralyses me.

The procession of the passing moments
Fails to achieve the soul's prayer of poor me
The hunger in my stomach.
And despondency in those eyes.

Would it rain today
Will the joy & restiveness of the drops of melody
and the refrain of dreams
Be heard ??

Sometimes year after year
obliges us to carry the corpses of the end of satiety
On our shoulders
& walk miles & miles.

The sky is cloudless today
And so was yesterday
The hues of desire & emotion
love & longing
The flowers of life
As if the sun is pinned like a pair of helpless nails
On earth's four walls.

Duryodhan

Behold yet
How intensely the foliage bewails
And the sight of dry leaves dropping
Like the last adieu
The wan, pallid spring.

All the kinsfolk & clan
lose their identity
The village club & gymnasium
The pomp & ceremony & vanity

The date palm branches
Look like a desperate
pitiless desert
The thicket of thorns & the exhausted camels
The birds unknown
Are your last inheritance.

The accumulated vanity
and strength of limbs
keeps mecting
like the Kaspian lake
in global warming.
The unseated arrogance
The ties of affection
The travellers by the last coffin

The skies of abode
Your soul gazes at the untimely rains of love.

Can you recall that game of chess
of deceit
The stripped body of a woman
The unrequited indulgence
Beauty & pageantry.

The river of blood
The plaintive beating of the heart
Shrieks & wailing
The shivered head, the splintered genitals
Legs, feet & nose
Neither the shore nor the shelter
Alone and alone
There is Duryodhan.

Love has died
Five villages prayed for
The recalcitrance of refusing
the earth measuring
the point of a needle.
The overweening arrogance
The vileness of insulting
the truth & Dharma.

Only tears are left
Palmfuls of disconsolate weeping
As the last resources
The broken, shattered pride
The ultimate stratagem
for wrapping up a life.

Flowers of stone

Whipping up the silence
It breaks its stubbornness
Its unyielding tricks
Flowers bloom in word after word
And life throbs in the point of
hammer & anvil.

It carves the flesh & bone inside the stone
blood flows & colour
The ravishing youth of the elfin maidens
And a thousand Eros hold them in thrall
As they worship the body beautiful.

The flowers would bloom
and spread their fragrance
And the love in stone
would seduce the being.

The saws & anvil scythe the stone
like pointed sword
A hundred thousand blow, wounds
in the stone

The pieces of stone that drop
Soak the body in drops of blood

And when the soul is drenched
The heart's inner abode is bloodied.

The labour room builds itself
In a spasm of high confidence
The mind & heart are intoxicated with beauty
A flower is born in the stone guileless.

Whether in stone or in earth
To make a flower blossom in faith
To draw a painting on the wall
or the canvas
As to the self-same imagination
Is no less than worshipping gods.

An Evening in the city

The evening descends
Like defrauding its lights
Crossing the uneasy
Smog & commotion
and the carts of chatwallah
Mandakini rearranges her attire
Locks & body
Spies into the mirror
with a backward look
And wears a smile
Muses how the life
paints a broken, opposite tide.
The sinking rays
fall aslant
beyond hills & tall palm trees
And the lofty high-rise
The stadium gallery
The city's last lamppost

The train whizzes its way
blowing horns
And who knows, who cares
for who enters the city
in the evening.

The river banks, the suburbs
The sickly banian tree
All draped in grey
In the blows of the wood smith's anvil
The twilight dark
Evening creeps in like a camel
treading its languorous feet.
Neon and highmast
The lamppost
Get extinguished ever so slowly
from the neighboring zones.
The dark face that looks like the eventide
In the shackled,
In the shackled, barred breasts of the city.
Promises & pretensions
New forms of speecwification & schemes
Get printed.

The River mirrors the sky

Right above your head
The sky you see
Is a river of dreams.

The water flows
Some delicate fingers
Work the swing
The stars of waves.

The coyness rippling beneath the lips
The timid touch of moonshine
The myriad coloured butterflies
flap the wings & fly away
A most beauteous sight.

Come, we would be unison,
The banks, waves & the boatman's song
Together with the
Stars, the moon & the sky.

River mirrors the sky
And is imaged in the sky's eyes.

The same emotion
The same redolence
The self-same love & affections
Whether you look for it
In the sky or in the river.

The eyes of Dark

The beautiful dark
That rises from the legends of darkness
like this darkling
The shadows of silence
That ooze out of darkness
Like silver eyes of same graceful maiden.

Dark and moon play hide & seek
Shadow beckon it to catch them
if it can.

The whole of the relationship in a dazzle
When the dense dark kisses it
The bonds between life & faith
between love & longing.

Dark can see everything
Truth & deceit.
What is writ on its walls
And what is wiped clean.

Where rocks of broken bones pile
The river of tears
The documents of self surrender
Of the innocent humanity.

It would be a long while
before the day breaks
but it can see everything
inside out.

It builds up an empire
through its detached look
The truth enduring
And you can see the face of light
in the deep, deep dark.

Cuttack

The ancient blacksmith
drags a long pull in his bidi
and lights up his fireplace.
from the tiny cabin in the narrow by lanes
The smoke curls up
The curls climb up
this way or that
to the right & the left.
The yellow sun traverses
hills & rivers
And descends from the treetops.
The red & blue flowers.

The streets get clogged with smog
Life lends it the company
The grey dirt piles up
like factory & flourmill
The dun thick coats
Amid the morning that dreams of the morrow.

The harsh sun wanes
The familiar sun of several days
gets wan
The shadow & light steadily retreat
In the scarlet sky

And yonder rises the dread
of an imminent storm
And the sun clambers across
the river & the earth.

The dark creeps from Bidanasi side
If you walk on the stone embankment
You came a cross
the Barabati Ramparts.
And Ravenshaw college, too.

The lamps on the streets
Suddenly cave a live
And so many chambers & minds
light up

The dense heaps of dark get etched
Against the low-lying areas
and on the opposite side
of the town
There were many a night
gets pregnant
beholding sins & promises.

The schemes & speeches
Take birth there
Each morning when the old blacksmith
lights up his fireplace
taking a full on his bidi
The rickety wooden cabin
Gives way with its
uneven wielding
And worms eat them up.

The Rain storm

The whole zone is dishevelled.
The stubborn claws of storm
Have sucked everything away
from the heart of earth
all the happiness, all the plainness

Trees, houses & hovels
all demolished.
And hearts, too, have broken.
The sparks of light have
disappeared.
And every soul weeps.

The ceaseless rain
The world, all over, is panicked.
The fount of living is suspended.
Rice & salt washed away
And so, too the idiom of life.
The unremitting down pour
And the whole district is inundated.

The flood of rain
Has wiped out
all the possibilities of living
All the joy
and
All the document.

Jharana Pothala

Time's festering cell
Sighing deep from beneath
the sibs of breast
You are burning crimson today.
 The mind breaks, losing dreams & faith.
 Embracing the half-burnt memories
and undisciplined squad of emotion
While lips ripple
into the wisps of a smile.

Looking at you attire
your gait & style
 In Banalata's & Alaka's land
You flash across my memory.
Pratima and Chandra Beherani.
I try to measure your
Vital statistics
Colour & elevation
I recall your amour, your lusciousness
Your face lowered
tying your tresses
And close to me
You rise & stand two feet away
Beneath those vacant vision
 A composed, but tired nerves

Of a dead morning.
The exhausted idioms of
long, thin fingers
Your saree, locks & bracelet
Weave into a curvature
Like the protruding breasts of Sila Apa.
Inside the class room,
near the college square
In a thatched hovel close to
Farida basti
I met you last evening
And we meet daily
At stenos cubicle, near the counter
and in Headquarters office.
Today is 'Utkal Divas'.
There would be roll call of merit
of proficient debaters
or those with spectacular
histrionics
they would receive so many awards
 from the minister.
And suddenly, the load shedding
And the night's insignia imprinted
on your body & clothing.
Your image gets plashed in photos
In close up.
In stylish prose, sensual
And someone else's breast, someone else's
lips & eyes focused
In the splintered mirror.

Your hands & feet
Get worn, sore & tired
Like yesterday
A heavy sadness descends
You keep painting in agony & dejection.
And seal those love letter's in blue envelops.
Who are you in love with, again?
A lot of chatting here
About your beauty, merit & habits.
Some say you are the black ant,
the venomous caterpillar!
The evening star beats its glow
against your blossoming grace.
The flow of a fount.
The still, unruffled sea
breaks into a tremble
Blue eyes darting from
under the burkha
The hermit as if, is seeking
the nirvana.
Prays for the body and the soul
The union of flesh
gesticulating meaningfully.
You keep repeating - I love you
And I love not.
You are an incomprehensible sum,
You are and you are not.
And you come to search with
decorous fingers
Your sense of pride & respectability.
And some such thing-
the quiet living.

The ravaged Noakhali
Muddied your flesh with sins
But today, your kind & being
Is a-shaken, fleeting
under the restless high
The earth under your feet
Metaphors of your impurity
Is that your identity!

Surrender

I would, rather, swallow all my tears
And suppress the overwhelming
gasps of sobbing
And the terms I refuse to yield
And brimming passion.

All those happiness & suffering
blood & tears
Would hunt out all the darkness
 in her terrain
and life's fragrance
And locate their details
Your benedictions
Would pluck them in jubilation
with folded palms
And offer me to myself
Your proffered oblations
your love & empathy.

Though I would feel desperate
And nobody to respond to my pleas
Everything would be reduced
to gibberish
This ancient, infirm, soundless life.
You would get tired searching

for the exit
And gulp all the unendurable pain
You would, too, measure the sea's depth
perching on the verandah
All and all the dimensions of the sky
And evaluate the soul
with a quiet undertone.

A poet Asks

Sometimes when I recline quietly
With a vacant mind
a pregnant pause
on my couch
I can observe from the roof of a
Quarters opposite me
 A devil's night loses its way
Every day
Inebriated, splurging on drinks
And awakens to reveal
her very own stories.

A below still hour
on the back of an unkempt road
A body ravaged sprawled
at the foot of a light post
Watched over by a murky moon
Clouded sky & stray bulls
The dark asphalt slumbers like a
horrible serpent
A bunch of thugs of the fearful dark
tear her flesh & entrails.

Would it lie there among dust & earth
beneath the lamppost
The dark moon & the cloudcapped sky
Would feast their eyes everyday
On her denuded chastity
everyday
in rapture !

Redolence

Evening and her dark
The flowery embrace
The scent of blossoms
floats in the woods' abandon
Longing for dreams
Licking the density of longing.

The flowers & their fragrance
Are so intimate
so familiar
Mind like a lively lamb
Is entrapped in its spider's web.

You look so lovely
and so do he waves of the naked sea.
And when you scamper to the shore
& hug those dry sands
And if you unclasp the intimacy
and strip her of the saree
 All the morality burns away
Body hungers for the body
for its closed in warmth
And the scent bewitches them
All the sea & the sky.

Two metaphors of love

The heart that easily melts
The desperate, anguished moans of love
Longs for a lonely moment
an intimate point.
Two souls remain wordless
And measure themselves
& their respective world
The dreams enraptured
In a fit of ecstasy
Plumbing the depths of emotion.

One who is living only for a moment.
Light & shadow
Love that lasts two days
Vanishing so soon.
They weigh the axis of relationship
In the contract   charter
& balance sheet.
Love is measured in profit & loss
And it ceases with exchange done.

The rights are sold here
In the mean bylanes & pavement
Reduced to romance counterfeit
In terms of flesh

Making love to still bodies
The poor helpless lass is bought and sold
Her body bearing the insignia
of agency & tender.

And love is approached in the canal colony
That sprawls like a slumbering python.
And he is about to plant a kiss
on those lips smacked
with lipstick
The affluent, chic lips
And then he retreats putting on
his shoes unobtrusively
And utters words
with clenched teeth
and in whispers.
As the words are formed
they disappear
On the lover's lips.

Night

The dark bunch of clouds creep
And sink their feet.
Swallow the day's rays & anxiety,
Clinging itself
to the dark fortnight's moon.

The confluence of all the nocturnals
Sleep & stars
slowly assemble in the sky
And the illusion of solace & respite.

The giant night that lies prostrate
Gets wild oftentimes
And its borders become quiet
Lays its head in earth's lap.
The still being throbs exuberantly
The depth of feelings
appear in the bemused being.

As the night descends
The flowers blow
And the chakor couple makes love
And play the minstrelsy.
The unknown fowls & the grasshoppers
Sing unceasingly.

Night wakes up with dreams
And as it closes
Embraces all the pride
of lovers & regrets.

The Goddess

Who may be the goddess
The question overwhelmed me
And held my body in coils
Soaking the mind entire
And aching the sensibility
for moments together.
Seeking a riposte
Who may it be.

One who has not yet grasped
the import of virtue or vice
In hunger & privation
Or what is sacred & profane
Who has sold out her
body & mind & rights
to an intermediary
In exchange of a kilo of rice
or two pieces of roti
She who is questing for her
Whereabouts & identity
May not she be a goddess !

That dark-skinned wench
Selling her wares on the footpath.
Who picks up the cowdung

And sells her fish
The fisherwoman Rama
She also is a goddess.

And that maiden
who has salvaged her life
in blood & tears
Spending the remainder of her life
as a gang raped victim
And withstood all the pains
like a slab of iron one
Is she not one !

And she baked in the searing
heat of the sun
for assembling her possible happing
And drenched in mud & slush
Has been able to reap
the golden harvest
Is she not a goddess !

And she must be the one
who has split her womb
to give birth to you
And pieced up the life
in drops of tear & blood
And is given to shower her blessings
May you grow old, very old.

Of me

Whether one follows it or not
I know my needs, my search.
I dip beneath the seven depths of slush
every day
Looking for the casket of life
This, of course, is my own,
Very own business.

The last arrogance & pluck
Slowly yields
The body gets aggrieved
tearing the easy self
I go searching in the thick
wilderness
for love & romance.

My sorrows are being talked about
in public
within & without
The grief's, like a worm,
eat into the entrails
in course of Karma.
There is nothing to eat,
no one to attend
But the body's indulgence wakes

like a tide in the full moon
eating into either banks of time.

Somebody goes looking for elephants or horses
Someone for pearls & diamonds
& water in the oasis
or searching for love in a
red-light bend
or looking for a good, happy soul,
But I go for the barest minimum,
the paltry means for a livelihood.

I pine for a straight road to subsist
Would it be easy finding the rare earth
a morsel of salt
a cup of rice-water
or a drop of the leftover !

The assured happiness eludes me
Everywhere the pretence & betrayals
fake & violence & deceit
If kamsa ordains
A hundred would be fated like me
to suffer the death.

The Role

How do I escape this very moment
Into the hidden woods surreptitiously
Like a fugitive.

Is it a moment for breaking up
In the salad days of youth
fresh & blooming
When so much of dreams &
 Possibilities sprout.

I have got to live upto my role
whatever is chosen for me
by others
The role that befits me.

I have to act it out firm
my mind & senses
& sensibility
And Power of judgement & faith.

Sowing the seeds of belief
In the breeze that
wafts across
In the wet darkness of dawn
Amid truth that boldly stares.

Then to redistribute
Life's overwhelming
Fragrance
And rearraign the personal effects
In a dishevelled house.

And also to situate
the happiness & self –belief
Light & solace
In an affectionate brace.

The Unknown Man

Where could we weigh
So many of them
their humanness
and the greatness of their humanity ?

Nor could we understand
the hunger in their stomach
the inner working of their mind
And the bosom's intimacy !

When did we grasp
that they are our own, very own
So much of love embedded in their being
Their desperate longing
to make us their own.

Equally difficult
to locate their habitation
The idiom   of their love
& the ease of their dialect.
He wishes us well
again & again, in bursts.
Closing his heart to us
Lest a bunch of darkness
Creeps into his soul for us.

Not born of blood
Yet closer than blood relation
Like kith & kin, the closest
nearer than ever.

We can find them
in the bylanes & slums of the city
In the hamlets at the foothills
In the fields & mining terrain
Away the cornfields &
faithful territories.

Time for Building

Let this earth
the sons of the soil
and the deluded morning
Be liberated from violence &
hatred & pain.

Let the blood soaked staff
be lowered down
from the fortress
of suffering
and the iron chains.

If you want to wake up
Open your mouth
The crisis of hunger & raiment.

Let us interrupt the false festivities
of the masked men around
and their confluence.

Build up whatever is lacking
An even passage
A colour that appeals to everybody
The unadulterated love
dear to all humanity.

Offering

The red hot eyes are so famished,
so devouring & so sharp
I felt his groping fingers prying
meticulously the body entire
All the nooks & crevices of limbs
the tresses, locks & forehead.

Not a single space escapes
his stare
Be it the back & lines of underbelly
All the sensitive glands
Are on search by his piercing vision.

And he tears my salwar, the seven folds of
my saree
Tearing them to pieces, smithereens
And splinters the stem, flowers & buds
Of the soft body in his canine tooth
And unveils the nether robes
the secret, wrapped composition of body.

The sharp, miniscule gaze
the sharpened teeth,
the sinful claws
bloodies the soft, delicate flesh

of Nirbhaya
And sometimes the maidens' objective faith
Seeks to measure the sinfulness
the maleness & guts of those glances
of the one who has created
those eyes ??

I feel like asking,
the things that keep me burning
in accumulated anger
His lustfulness, the lingering sensuality
I would unfold me-come, you, come
who intend to ravish me.

And suck from my vagina
all the longing, curiosity
whatever you want
all the fevers of the body
And summon them that would follow you
In denuding me & having their fill
who seek pleasure in me
All of you, come, have your fill,
till I last
till I endure
And let this loathsome act close
here & now.

Descending unto the Earth

I am counting stars in the vacancy of waiting
And measuring the moonlight
About your arrival here.

Please carry a palmful of joy
While descending unto the earth
And scatter, a bunch of peace here
The woods, hills & meadows
river, seas & skies
Would wash in the seven hues
of happiness
In human mind.

Enfold a sheaf of rays
in the hem of your saree
And spread them in my
Consciousness.
from village to cities
In all the sensibilities
The darkness would melt
and the light's current
would flow
In every life.

For the sake of mother's love
Bring while coming
a pick of virtue,
a palmful of Dharma
A thick of bondage
& a drop of affection.

While parting, bestow
all your benedictions
In joyful recompense
And import as much as possible
all the courage & strength
to countenance the Sins & pretensions
and to brave all the sorrows
& hunger
& privations.

No clouds in the sky

Just tell me
About the scene of my inner self
how it has been pointed.
In the sensual green
or in the parched, grey
Spread of sands.

How do the four skylines look
the lines of my brow
The earth beneath my feet
The pair of engrossed eyes.

Hear me, O dwellers of the cities
the lotus of love blossoms no more
And hardly a stir in the breeze
And the green woods are invisible.

Death beckons me
and dreams, too
Life harkens me back
And pain calls me
The smog & dust ridden skies
lacerate me.

My supplications have not

reached   these moments
that have passed
And the hunger in my stomach
And the hunger in my stomach
And the despondency
in my eyes.

Would it rain today.
And would the joy & desperation
be heard in the cadence of dream
And the lilt in the patter of rains.
Sometimes, year after year
I am obliged to carry the corpses
on my shoulders
at the journey's end
To walk miles together.

Today, sky has no clouds
like yesterday
Nor the colour of desire & passion
Love & expectation
The flowers of life
As if the cruel, wretched sun
has planted two hard nails
Into the four walls of
the earth.

Passer-by

Although I promise to walk
Traversing a long distance
Till the end page of life
is folded
Till the light dies out.

Look at these feet
resisting all there is to resist
What impertinence (in them)
Tired as they are treading
And they are fervid yet
to move forward.

It leaves nothing to surmise
I have got to cover
miles after miles
The crooked curves & bends & crevices
On the uneven asphalt
and slushy tracks
Strewn with pebbles.

Once I have stepped out
can you ever steady
those obstinate feet
They are bursting to walk away
a long, long time.

If everybody could walk this way
even while alone
Looking for a mint fresh morning
and a breath of pristine air.

Though I fancy
& they came true sometimes
I may chance upon some upright ones
So suddenly,

A dainty image of morning
The salad earth
& the dearest of the time
invoking love.

Ascension

On a fresh, livid evening
And into a river of innocence
I threw away all the sorrows
and today's anguish.

Evening lent a fulfilling confluence
And had a pact with the night
They would wash away
all the hesitancy
and dejection on lips
Floating away in the opposite current
So far
Skies, stars & moon
& dear, dear night
Moonlight soaked my being.

Clouds were in the sky
Had an eyeful of dreams
And I plucked the warmth
Caressing the rainy lips.

The heart was entranced
in so much of beauty & happiness
The river, the moon & the rains
The sky & the dark

The soul awakens suddenly
in rapture.

No storm in the skies & the earth
My mind fails to register
the mutinous heat
Senses grow indolent & placid
On the edges of consciousness.

Life beckons to lose its way
For eternity
Into the folds of earth & skies
The seven seasons of mind
The sweetness of the
unforgettable memory.

Poetry : Thou Hast no peers

You wake up bemused
in a mantra
And keep painting images
of weal & woe.

Everything gets inscribed
of its own accord
Every image & character.
Virtue & vice, justice & retribution
And in terms of mystery
Spanning cradle & grave.

You can make the flowers bloom
And create rains
And can write many a poem
of life and death .

There is so much joy
when I get lost
Dreams of ocean
You are sans peer
In all the agony that burns.

Your soul loses its way,
gets immersed

for ever.
And merges into fathomless hope
 Like the radiant sky
Like earth's fragrance
Enraptured in the ultimate hour.

The sunken & indrawn longing
& aspiration
The menstrual night
The refulgent day
Blossoms like flowers
In terms of my emotion within
Thou art my love.

The Sunlight

Palmfuls of sunlight
Ship from my limbs to yours
The steaming light & shadow
Dance on the asphalt
& overblown cornfields
And the elusive mirage dances
Swinging its buttocks.

The baked trees & foliage
from the earth's rim to the skies
Around the woods & fields
As if an angry serpent
keeps dancing with fangs unfurled.

Summer's cruel heat whips
the back & belly
& tears it apart.
And dry wind blows around
Everything trapped
in a poacher's machinations
Concrete jungle & the petrol smoke.

Dear chum, let's today
look for green delight
Youth's blossoms in the ravaged body.

Seeking love in leaves & stalk
Storing the pride of building
a roof over head, and an umbrella
In a night of courage
Let the trees become
a happy dream from
The heat of the oven.

Death

Death does me in
day in, day out
In so many kinds.
In so many fashions.
And I die these days
in novel modes.

The frenzied limbs
The bloodied toes & the skin
underneath
Seeking a secure nook
I go questing for a way out.

I go gathering
disillusionment & fraud
In my beak
And I eat them up tearing their entrails
in the sharp beak.
I die & wake up into life again
On the pretext of what virtue
or stratagem.

I burn my body
& assemble my soul
Putting a slab on my breast

I chanced upon my end
once again.

The broken wall & ruined crops
As I look at the face of
the pallid skies
The earth beneath my feet gives way.
I die, I live
I live and die again
And continue to watch
Life & luck
day in, day out.

Silence

Not a stir of breeze
unlike yesterday.
No cadence of words.
Everywhere an angry silence
The lonely shadows & disguised colours
All quiet
The mango orchard, the river bank
The tiny hamlet at the
foothills.
The cowherd boy plays the flute.

Soundless sky
The shrill twitter of grasshopper
The commotion of the woodcutters
Splitting the wood.
The chowkidar yells – 'beware'.
Everything reduced to silence
As if we're in for a spell of
disillusionment.
The moon spreads its lazy beams
The hills are sere rocks
And here & there
Trees stand shorn of foliage.
Timid & helpless.

One knows not why this
thick dark
No complaint, nor riposte.
Woods & hills
Men, intelligent & idiot
Everything blank
Everybody tense, soundless
The silent man plays his games
In Time's bed of sands.

Seven Rounds to a Dream

I sowed a bunch of seeds
The sprouting paddy
Palmfuls of virile faith.

In a night that looked white
like a blossom
It was agreed to
In the company of a quiet time
I would be in a sexual congress
& keep planting
Those pristine embrace
The house of romance
was built
In the fresh dark of a
Pousha night.

I met Lili in a scorching midday
While stone pelting
at mango branches
And she implored-let us
be companions for seven lives
I knew not when we
indulged in lovemaking
She, the bony lass & me
all through the night

The tides of the sea washed away
all the filth off my body
And the dry beach got wet.

The moon & stars took
alibi of exhaustion
From the lotus pool was heard
The bemused melody of a
Connoisseur
The immaculate couch
got soaked in the
conceits of indulgence.
The girlie of shyness
that was recondite.

The imaged aspiration
In the repetitive menstruation
of myriad longing.
I saw, at an instant,
my mother's womb
And fought with death for a moment
And put up absurd queries
in the naked infancy.
Coming across a host of
events & mishaps
Memories & oblivion
retreated of their own.

The consummation of seasons
The bonding of rains & cloud
As I gazed at the ovary
of trees, founts & rivers

And there lay a profusion of festivities
Of Prakriti & Purusha.

I was nettled in the dark
Having seen all those sufferings,
the perceived menace
The dreams jostling all around
Dreams blew & drenched me
Folds of them wrapping me
all through the night.

Irony

I was to beg
one foot of earth
a handful of affections
the brimming emotion.

I wanted to beg a sliver of sky
iust a glance of love
fragrant & palmful.

I sought a brimful of dream
hopes in a palm
and a bunch of lyrical romantic poesy.

I was praying for a hymn
of benediction
love from the corner of the heart
and wanted the remainder of the day
to be like the redolence
of zephyrus.

But what could I ask
except palmful of darkness & regrets
Vanity & jealousy
The wounded agonized living
Sensibility & fugitive dream.

Mask

I can barely speak all the truth
for I dread somebody or other
within me.
Sometimes I conceal myself
in disguise
how long would this fun continue !

The earth is moist with tears
And the sky in mourning
The trees & creepers & hills
Are catalogued in a deadly
annunciation.

This concealment may be
more horrible than death.

O poet, sharpen your words
and enkindle the consciousness
May the craft of unsheathing the
arrow be more skillful.

We have to liberate ourselves
from this dread,
this illusion
from the confines of
this dark coffin.

Strip the veil
and converted from the language
And unmask the disguised face
O you, second god.
Are you listening !

Identity

I have already sighted my fate
recessed in Time's headlines
from a close up
It feels cruel and yet
my very own.

The struggling life
The revolution the roads &
in the sprawling slums.
I have found so much of ideology
The stripping of their truth & falsity
The way ahead chequered
by light and dark
The high hills & swamps.

My bones have sea weed in them
and dice in my skin
alcohol in my viscera.
The arrogance & vanity
make a jig
like a headless body
with the intoxication of youth.

My destiny, my god
are buried beneath

the slab of a stone.
Life in the morning & evening
is of a moment to moment
in installment.

I'm Nityanand, if you did not know
from Patnagarh village
And I keep yelling today
like yesterday
Inquilab zindaband

Destination

I asked them all
The morning birds
The sun & the seas
And asked my grandma
How far is my destination ?

I made a pact with
breeze & lofty hilltops
with the stellar sky
with an supplication
let me into if you know
how far is my destination.

I have arranged everything
cavalry & elephants
The conveyance & fleet
And the utmost strength allowable
The inevitable expedition
To seek the passage of my dreams.

The trackless woods &
undergrowth
Full of thorns & this les,
And perhaps barren, uphill storms & high winds
And the clique of scheming psychophants.

I would travel the same road
where dreams pile
and wealth of possibilities
accumulate
Where there is food for the hungry
and empathy of one for the other.

Cover

Traversing times sand bridges
You have covered rivers & ravines
& human habitation
Fields hills & hamlets.
And you have overcame
the regrets & vanity
making this body
this mind a plaintiff.

Sometimes to evade your gaze
from the frailties
You have resorted to companies
& sympathies
In a shrewd move.

You have attired so many
eyes skies & love
and palms of your feet
In new apparel.
Defining new roles for them.

So often you've silenced yourself
Lest truth reveals itself
In your scar let eyes & cruelty
Like a pore in the eyes & face
So much of gestures & postures.

You have forgotten so many things
That you have an instinct
and animal passions
& also glories.

And sought so many times
The darkness of secret recesses
Like a snails cloak
& snakeskin
to conceal the appropriation
of inanimate clothes.

The spectacles

It happens to be my lot
When my glasses break down
Or get displaced
I am wont to lose my way
It's so ordained.

The age no more abides
the makers of destiny
Of visible & invisible universe
There is a scene change
In the low-lying soil or
half-soil
In the clayey mud.

My lenses are my destiny,
my support
It keeps in with the sunrise of marrow
Carrying the parallel price
of the incomparable jewel

If I intend to probe into the past
and if it is needed
I can see it
as I take down my glasses
Sans impediment, sans effort.

My age outstrips my youth
and finds beneath the curtains
of my looking glass
well-nigh correctly
life's desired location,
of its remainder.

You may say it is replete
With affection
or so intimate
or it is perhaps a sentimental
walking stick
I climb the ladder of spectacles
& dismount in the staircase
I keep playing life's game
of ladder & snake.

The face across the windows

When I open the casement
The gay abandon of the
murmuring breeze
The remote horizon is in the offing.

The sky turns erotic, sensual
Touching the earth, eyes & the
brim of the heart
And I see there a face :
The spoilt face the kings & queens
brought up
The face staring like a rising sun.

Flowers bloom
Their redolence overwhelming
the lips & buttocks
Like a close-up embrace
They wrap up the consciousness
The colour scatters

Trudging the fount of the threshold
The sun caresses
the tall deodars & the summit of the highrise
and sands of the sea
As the cowdust hour settles

the stars get immersed
in moonshine.

Whoever quested for the passage
traversing tall branches, hills &
lampposts
imploring love
and laying for dreams that linger
The sight is bewitching in my eyes
playing hide & seek
across the windows.

As I looked back

As I looked back
I saw the dwindling footprints
The fading drops of tears
life's watercolour
My engrossed quiet.

As I stared back
I spied behind me
The frescoed festoons of emotion
The faint chirpings
And some intimacy, some querries
About Misery & happiness.

As I gazed back
I found the ruptured moments of life
floating in the reverse current
Touching Time's lyricism
ironically twisted.

As I longed back
I found heaps of bitter alliteration
of life's strifes & agonies
piling from back to back
The fatuous synopsis of the
remainder of hopes.

Although it is inscribed
in page after page
The many-hued blossoms of life
A few white
And the remaining grey, pearly
They are dear to me yet
Annals of love in the
flashback.

The Afternoon sky

Dreams bloom & wither away
In my eyes nowadays
That are like the eyes of this afternoon

All the paintings I did paint
& do today
Straining my fingers
In the buried being
Breaking my bones
Pouring for the blood & tears
They all are wiped clean
With an indolent temper.

I saw the sad, forsaken sun
Sets out of time
In ruptured longings
tearing the bowels of horizon.

I am hardly fortynine
approaching the fiftieth
The night has not ended yet
The dreams remain to be dreamt
The way lies unwalked
My love is not fulfilled yet.

The sky looks pallid though
Spreading to the rims of horizon
Dust & smoke & birds twitter-
fill it in
The series of regrets & helplessness.

And yet this sky
touches the light
spreads the hue
And brings the expectation to bloom
Dreams keep painting
the fresh footprints of time.

Obeisance

A pristine feeling
Can build a Konark of words
And a Taj Mahal of emotions.

A cold trepidation
Lengthens like a fountain
of even length
The words sparkle like
Stars in the sky.

I mope about the bed restive
Wakeful throughout the night
And I wake up to her soft caress
As I turn sides.

He overwhelms me
Like a sprightly rivulet
The dense, thick woods
and the hills that kiss the sky.

I will have to give those back
the miscellaneous temptation
The noble wealth of regal ceremony
I beg like an ascetic
A palmful of phrases.

My heart beats eloquent
The sexual congress of words
Became embodied in mind.

The iron fence gives way
from under the feet
The words play hide & seek
Sans a care
And love blossoms in the sky.

I am amazed at this
intimate spectacle
Its impenetrable aim
transfixes me
And the wound bleeds
The blood becomes the flower
And the lotus of idiom.

The free untrammelled words
distribute colour
into the fresh blown dreams.
The carpet of tears glowing
in your memory
And the desperate yearning
failing to find poetry.

And sometimes the sun rises
As the language sends
the blowing of conchshell
The butterflies shaking their wings
The light sweeps
And I pay obeisance
unto thee.

An Autobiography

Whether one understands it or not
I know my sense of need
Going under seven layers of slush
each day
To find the mythical casket of life
It remains my very own
stuff of life.

Sometimes I admit defeat
Sundering the ultimate pride
& the identity of an
obdurate innocence
The body lacerated
While the pair me goes looking for
Love & parbion
in the wilderness of woods.

Everybody wakes about my misery
within or without my home
I suffer like a worm
Eking out my incessant and
as Karma ordains.
Neither food nor attendant
The sensual pleasures aggravate
like a tide in the full-blown moon

touching time's either bank.

Somebody goes gathering elephant
or horses
or pearls & topaz
Searching for water in the oasis
Pining for love
in the harlot's lane
Hoping to see a kind soul
But I hope for a barest minimum
means of paltry existence

I need a straight path
for living
Would it be easy to acquire
a scarce space of earth
a spoonful of salt
a mouthful of rice water & water.

The easy happiness eludes
There is pretensions everywhere
retribution & violence
If Kamsa commands
there would be millions of death
& its like.

Debaki

The body gets merged in ever fresh tears
The stone walls
The iron threshold
bear their own weight
and give birth to a living god.

The hands, feet & life
are shackled
in myriad blows & anger of
a thousand yokes.

She has seen it so many times
thesnuffing of a hundred life & of truth
Her blind, irredeemable fate is in fetters
in a stone fortress.

Storm & rain besiege the city.
The river over flowing.
The thunder, lightning &kansa
To wipe Deaki's sorrows
& redeem kubja of her deformity
& the sins of kansa
A million means hold their
ground base firmly.

BLACK EAGLE BOOKS

www.blackeaglebooks.org
info@blackeaglebooks.org

Black Eagle Books, an independent publisher, was founded as a nonprofit organization in April, 2019. It is our mission to connect and engage the Indian diaspora and the world at large with the best of works of world literature published on a collaborative platform, with special emphasis on foregrounding Contemporary Classics and New Writing.

www.ingramcontent.com/pod-product-compliance
Lightning Source LLC
Chambersburg PA
CBHW031126080526
44587CB00011B/1135